# THE COMPLETE GESÙ Bambino

## (The Infant Jesus)
### by Pietro Yon

## NINE VERSIONS OF THE CHRISTMAS CLASSIC
## IN ONE VOLUME

MW00387150

Art Design: Jorge Paredes

# ABOUT THE COMPOSER

Pietro Alessandro Yon was born August 8, 1886, in Settimo Vittone, Italy. He studied at the Milan and Turin Conservatories of Music and later studied organ at the Santa Cecilia in Rome. For a time he was organist at St. Peter's in Rome before moving to the United States in 1907. Yon became a U. S. citizen in 1921. He became organist at St. Francis-Xavier in New York and then was appointed organist of St. Patrick's Cathedral in New York in 1926. He served this cathedral until his death, November 22, 1943.

Yon was considered a great organist, teacher, and composer. "Gesù Bambino," composed in 1917, remains his best-known work although he also wrote an oratorio, numerous instrumental pieces, masses, and other sacred works.

# CONTENTS

*to Francesca Pessagno with devotion and affection*

# GESÙ BAMBINO
## (The Infant Jesus)

High Voice in G

FREDERICK H. MARTENS

PIETRO A. YON

FEM00001

**Tempo I**

gain, __ the heart __ with rap - ture glows To greet the ho — ly night_____ That
*bel __ bam - bin __ non pian - ge - re, Non pian - ger Re - den - tor,_____ La*

gave __ the world __ its Christ - mas Rose, Its King __ of Love __ and Light._____ Let
*mam - ma tu - a cul - lan - do - ti Ti ba - cia, o Sal - va - tor._____ O -*

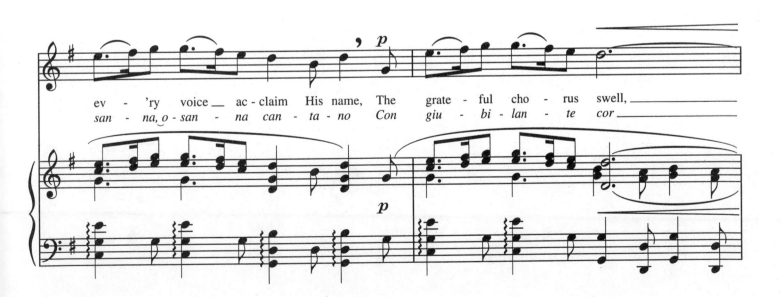

ev - 'ry voice __ ac - claim His name, The grate - ful cho - rus swell,_____
*san - na, o - san - na can - ta - no Con giu - bi - lan - te cor_____*

*to Francesca Pessagno with devotion and affection*

# GESÙ BAMBINO
### (The Infant Jesus)

Medium Voice in F

FREDERICK H. MARTENS

PIETRO A. YON

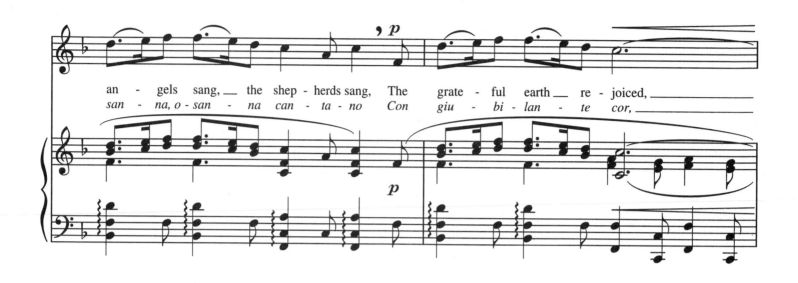

an - gels sang,___ the shep - herds sang, The grate - ful earth___ re - joiced,_____
*san - na, o - san - na can - ta - no Con giu - bi - lan - te cor,_____*

And at___ His bless - ed birth, the stars, Their ex - ul - ta - tion
*I tuoi___ pa - sto - ri ed an - ge - li O Re___ di lu - ce e a-*

voiced._____ O come let us a - do-
*mor_____ Ve - ni - te a - do-*

*All distinta violinista Maria Luisa Di Lorenzo*

# GESÙ BAMBINO

## Pastorale
### for Violin with Piano or Organ

PIETRO A. YON

VIOLIN

Violin - 2

**Tempo I**

gain, __ the heart __ with rap - ture glows To greet the ho - ly night _____ That
*bel __ bam - bin __ non pian - ge - re, Non pian - ger Re - den - tor, _____ La*

gave __ the world __ its Christ - mas Rose, Its King __ of Love __ and Light. _____ Let
*mam - ma tu - a cul - lan - do - ti Ti ba - cia, o Sal - va - tor. _____ O -*

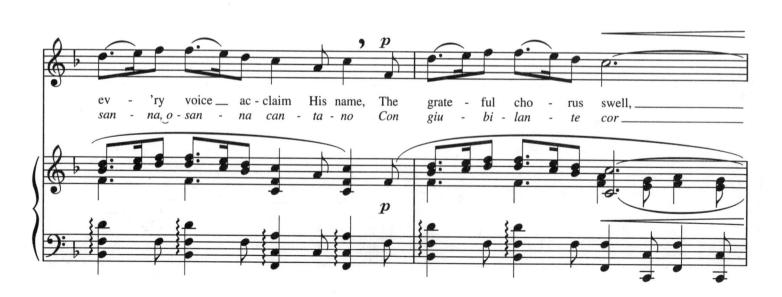

ev - 'ry voice __ ac - claim His name, The grate - ful cho - rus swell, _____
*san - na, o - san - na can - ta - no Con giu - bi - lan - te cor _____*

16

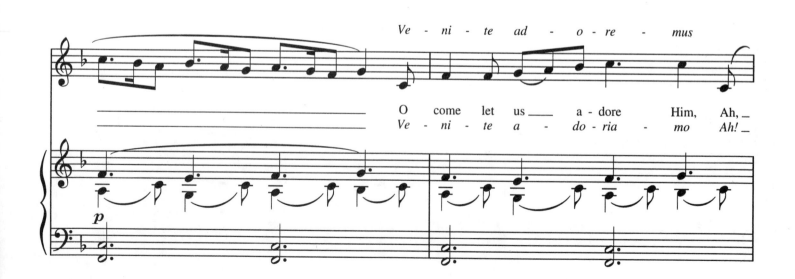

FEM00001

*to Francesca Pessagno with devotion and affection*

# GESÙ BAMBINO
## (The Infant Jesus)

Low Voice in E

FREDERICK H. MARTENS

PIETRO A. YON

an - gels sang, __ the shep - herds sang, The grate - ful earth __ re - joiced, __

*san - na, o - san - na can - ta - no Con giu - bi - lan - te cor,* __

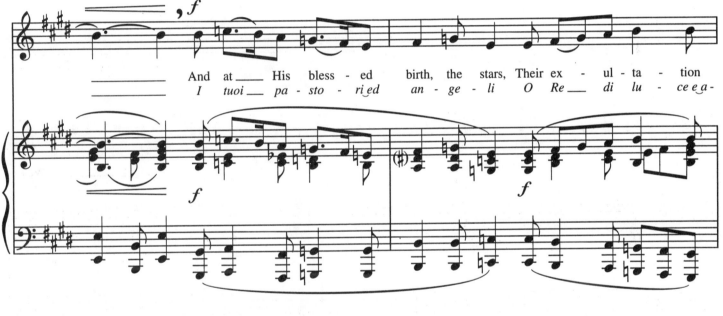

And at __ His bless - ed birth, the stars, Their ex - ul - ta - tion

*I tuoi __ pa - sto - ri ed an - ge - li O Re __ di lu - ce e a-*

**Non troppo lento**

*Ve - ni - te a - do -*

voiced. __ O come let us a-

*mor* __ *Ve - ni - te a - do -*

*sentito*

gain,__ the heart__ with rap - ture glows To greet the ho - ly night_____ That
*bel__ bam - bin__ non pian - ge - re, Non pian - ger Re - den - tor,_____ La*

gave__ the world__ its Christ - mas Rose, Its King__ of Love__ and Light._____ Let
*mam - ma tu - a cul - lan - do - ti Ti ba - cia, o Sal - va - tor._____ O -*

ev - 'ry voice__ ac - claim His name, The grate - ful cho - rus swell,_____
*san - na, o - san - na can - ta - no Con giu - bi - lan - te cor_____*

22

*Most respectfully inscribed to the Academy and College of Mount St. Vincent on the Hudson*

# GESÙ BAMBINO
## (The Infant Jesus)
### PASTORALE

PIETRO A. YON

FEM00001

**Non troppo lento**

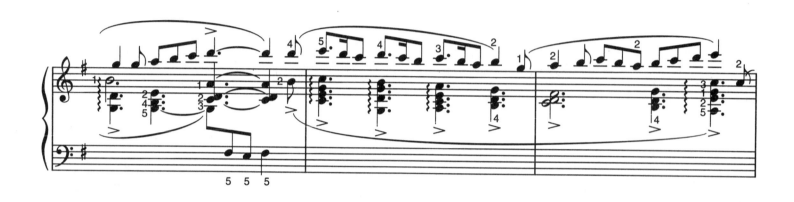

**Tempo I**

*al mio picolo tesoro Mario*

# GESÙ BAMBINO

### (The Infant Jesus)
### PASTORALE

PIETRO A. YON

**Andante mosso**

# GESÙ BAMBINO
## (The Infant Jesus)
### PASTORALE

PIETRO A. YON
*Arranged by BERNICE FROST*

*to Mr. Ralph Kinder, Philadelphia*

# GESÙ BAMBINO
(The Infant Jesus)
### PASTORALE

PIETRO A. YON

SW: Oboe 8'
GT: Chimes
CH: String and Celeste 8'
PED: Bourdon 16', Ch. to Ped.

FEM00001

38

**Poco meno**
Sw. off Oboe add Flute 8'

FEM00001

Sw. [off Flute 8'
add Oboe

*a tempo*

*rall.*

Ch.

Sw. ⌈ off Flute 8'
    ⌊ add Oboe

*a tempo*

**Tempo I**

Gt.

*p*

# GESÙ BAMBINO

SW: Oboe 8'
GT: Chimes
CH: String and Celeste 8'
PED: Soft 16', Ch. to Ped.

PIETRO A. YON
*Arranged as a duet*
*for Organ and Piano*
*by W.A. GOLDSWORTHY*

ORGAN

PIANO

Gt. (off chimes) add Prin. 8', Flutes 8', 4'

rall.

Gt. *f*

*a tempo*

rall.

*f* *a tempo*

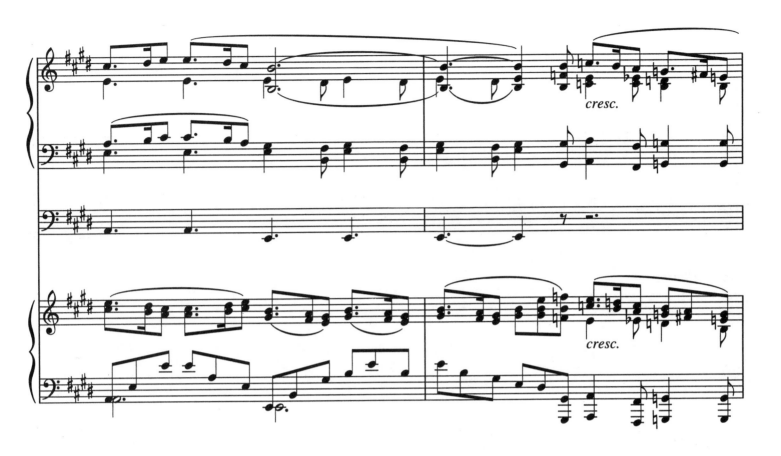

48

50

FEM00001

**Tempo I**

**Tempo I**

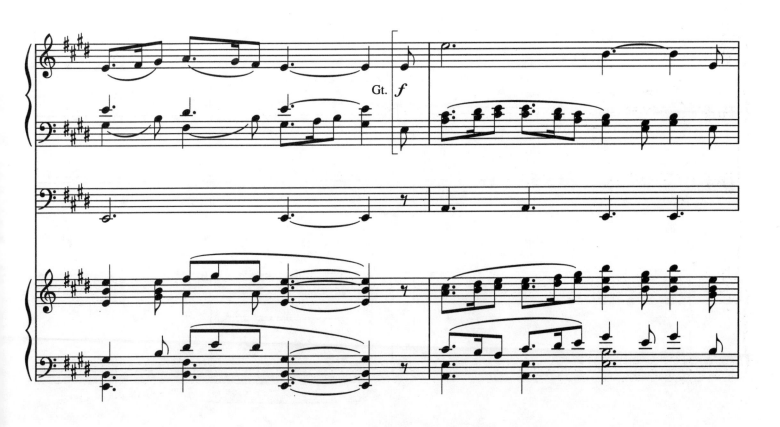

*All distinta violinista Maria Luisa Di Lorenzo*

# GESÙ BAMBINO

## Pastorale
## for Violin with Piano or Organ

PIETRO A. YON

\* In bars 3-6, and where passage is repeated, the melody in the accompaniment may be played on chimes.
The introduction may be treated in like manner.

60

61

FEM00001